# The Electoral College

# THE ELECTORAL COLLEGE

by

William C. Kimberling, Deputy Director
FEC Office of Election Administration

*(The views expressed here are solely those of the author and are not necessarily shared by the Federal Election Commission or any division thereof.)*

In order to appreciate the reasons for the Electoral College, it is essential to understand its historical context and the problem that the Founding Fathers were trying to solve. They faced the difficult question of how to elect a president in a nation that:

- was composed of thirteen large and small States jealous of their own rights and powers and suspicious of any central national government

- contained only 4,000,000 people spread up and down a thousand miles of Atlantic seaboard barely connected by transportation or communication (so that national campaigns were impractical even if they had been thought desirable)

- believed, under the influence of such British political thinkers as Henry St John Bolingbroke, that political parties were mischievous if not downright evil, and

- felt that gentlemen should not campaign for public office (The saying was "The office should seek the man, the man should not seek the office.").

How, then, to choose a president without political parties, without national campaigns, and without upsetting the carefully designed balance between the presidency and the Congress on one hand and between the States and the federal government on the other?

## Origins of the Electoral College

The Constitutional Convention considered several possible methods of selecting a president.

One idea was to have the Congress choose the president. This idea was rejected, however, because some felt that making such a choice would be too divisive an issue and leave too many hard feelings in the Congress. Others felt that such a procedure would invite unseemly political bargaining, corruption, and perhaps even interference from foreign powers. Still others felt that such an arrangement would upset the balance of power between the legislative and executive branches of the federal government.

A second idea was to have the State legislatures select the president. This idea, too, was rejected out of fears that a president so beholden to the State legislatures might permit them to erode federal authority and thus undermine the whole idea of a federation.

A third idea was to have the president elected by a direct popular vote. Direct election was rejected not because the Framers of the Constitution doubted public intelligence but rather because they feared that without sufficient information about candidates from outside their State, people would naturally vote for a "favorite son" from their own State or region. At worst, no president would emerge with a popular majority sufficient to govern the whole country. At best, the choice of president would always be decided by the largest, most populous States with little regard for the smaller ones.

Finally, a so-called "Committee of Eleven" in the Constitutional Convention proposed an indirect election of the president through a College of Electors.

The function of the College of Electors in choosing the president can be likened to that in the Roman Catholic Church of the College of Cardinals selecting the Pope. The original idea was for the most knowledgeable and informed individuals from each State to select the president based solely on merit and without regard to State of origin or political party.

The structure of the Electoral College can be traced to the Centurial Assembly system of the Roman Republic. Under that system, the adult male citizens of Rome were divided, according to their wealth, into groups of 100 (called Centuries). Each group of 100 was entitled to cast only one vote either in favor or against proposals submitted to them by the Roman Senate. In the Electoral College system, the States serve as the Centurial groups (though they are not, of course, based on wealth), and the number of votes per State is determined by the size of each State's Congressional delegation. Still, the two systems are similar in design and share many of the same advantages and disadvantages.

The similarities between the Electoral College and classical institutions are not accidental. Many of the Founding Fathers were well schooled in ancient history and its lessons.

## The First Design

In the first design of the Electoral College (described in Article II, Section 1 of the Constitution):

Each State was allocated a number of Electors equal to the number of its U.S. Senators (always 2) plus the number of its U.S. Representatives (which may change each decade according to the size of each State's population as determined in the decennial census). This arrangement built upon an earlier compromise in the design of the Congress itself and thus satisfied both large      and small States.

■ The manner of choosing the Electors was left to the individual State legislatures, thereby pacifying States suspicious of a central national government.

■ Members of Congress and employees of the federal government were specifically prohibited from serving as an Elector in order to maintain the balance between the legislative and executive branches of the federal government.

■ Each State's Electors were required to meet in their respective States rather than all together in one great meeting. This arrangement, it was thought, would prevent bribery, corruption, secret dealing, and foreign influence.

■ In order to prevent Electors from voting only for a "favorite son" of their own State, each Elector was required to cast two votes for president, at least one of which had to be for someone outside their home State. The idea, presumably, was that the winner would likely be everyone's second favorite choice.

■ The electoral votes were to be sealed and transmitted from each of the States to the President of the Senate who would then open them before both houses of the Congress and read the results.

■ The person with the most electoral votes, provided that it was an absolute majority (at least one over half of the total), became president. Whoever obtained the next greatest number of electoral votes became vice president -- an office which they seem to have invented for the occasion since it had not been mentioned previously in the Constitutional Convention.

■ In the event that no one obtained an absolute majority in the Electoral College or in the event of a tie vote, the U.S. House of Representatives, as the chamber closest to the people, would choose the president from among the top five contenders. They would do this (as a further concession to the small States) by allowing each State to cast only one vote with an absolute majority of the States being required to elect a president. The vice presidency would go to whatever remaining contender had the greatest number of electoral votes. If that, too, was tied, the U.S. Senate would break the tie by deciding between the two.

In all, this was quite an elaborate design. But it was also a very clever one when you consider that the whole operation was supposed to work *without political parties* and *without national campaigns* while maintaining the balances and satisfying the fears in play at the time. Indeed, it is probably because the Electoral College was originally designed to operate in an environment so totally different from our own that many people think it is anachronistic and fail to appreciate the new purposes it now serves. But of that, more later.

## The Second Design

The first design of the Electoral College lasted through only four presidential elections. For in the meantime, political parties had emerged in the United States. The very people who had been condemning parties publicly had nevertheless been building them privately. And too, the idea of political parties had gained respectability through the persuasive writings of such political philosophers as Edmund Burke and James Madison.

One of the accidental results of the development of political parties was that in the presidential election of 1800, the Electors of the Democratic-Republican Party gave Thomas Jefferson and Aaron Burr (both of that party) an equal number of electoral votes. The tie was resolved by the House of Representatives in Jefferson's favor -- but only after 36 tries and some serious political dealings which were considered unseemly at the time. Since this sort of bargaining over the presidency was the very thing the Electoral College was supposed to prevent, the Congress and the States hastily adopted the Twelfth Amendment to the Constitution by September of 1804.

To prevent tie votes in the Electoral College which were made probable, if not inevitable, by the rise of political parties (and no doubt to facilitate the election of a president and vice president of the same party), the 12th Amendment requires that each Elector cast *one* vote for president and a *separate* vote for vice president rather than casting two votes for president with the runner-up being made vice president. The Amendment also stipulates that if no one receives an absolute majority of electoral votes for president, then the U.S. House of Representatives will select the president from among the top three contenders with each State casting only one vote and an absolute majority being required to elect. By the same token, if no one receives an absolute majority for vice president, then the U.S. Senate will select the vice president from among the top two contenders for that office. All other features of the Electoral College remained the same including the requirement that, in order to prevent Electors from voting only for "favorite sons",  either the presidential or vice presidential candidate has to be from a State other than that of the Electors.

In short, political party loyalties had, by 1800, begun to cut across State loyalties thereby creating new and different problems in the selection of a president.  By making seemingly slight changes, the 12th Amendment fundamentally altered the design of the Electoral College and, in one stroke, accommodated political parties as a fact of life in American presidential elections.

It is noteworthy in passing that the idea of electing the president by direct popular vote was not widely promoted as an alternative to redesigning the Electoral College.  This may be because the physical and demographic circumstances of the country had not changed that much in a dozen or so years.  Or it may be because the excesses of the recent French revolution (and its fairly rapid degeneration into dictatorship) had given the populists some pause to reflect on the wisdom of too direct a democracy.

# The Evolution of the Electoral College

Since the 12th Amendment, there have been several federal and State statutory changes which have affected both the time and manner of choosing Presidential Electors but which have not further altered the fundamental workings of the Electoral College.  There have also been a few curious incidents which its critics cite as problems but which proponents of the Electoral College view as merely its natural and intended operation.

### The Manner of Choosing Electors

From the outset, and to this day, the manner of choosing its State's Electors was left to each State legislature.  And initially, as one might expect, different States adopted different methods.

Some State legislatures decided to choose the Electors themselves. Others decided on a direct popular vote for Electors either by Congressional district or at large throughout the whole State.  Still others devised some combination of these methods.  But in all cases, Electors were chosen individually from a single list of all candidates for the position.

During the 1800's, two trends in the States altered and more or less standardized the manner of choosing Electors.  The first trend was toward choosing Electors by the direct popular vote of the whole State (rather than by the State legislature or by the popular vote of each Congressional district).  Indeed, by 1836,  all States had moved to choosing their Electors by a direct statewide popular vote except South Carolina which persisted in choosing them by the State legislature until 1860.  Today, all States choose their Electors by direct statewide election except Maine (which in 1969) and

Nebraska (which in 1991) changed to selecting two of its Electors by a statewide popular vote and the remainder by the popular vote in each Congressional district.

Along with the trend toward their direct statewide election came the trend toward what is called the "winner-take-all" system of choosing Electors. Under the winner-take-all system, the presidential candidate who wins the most popular votes within a State wins all of that State's Electors. This winner-take-all system was really the logical consequence of the direct statewide vote for Electors owing to the influence of political parties. For in a direct popular election, voters loyal to one political party's candidate for president would naturally vote for that party's list of proposed Electors. By the same token, political parties would propose only as many Electors as there were electoral votes in the State so as not to fragment their support and thus permit the victory of another party's Elector.

There arose, then, the custom that each political party would, in each State, offer a "slate of Electors" -- a list of individuals loyal to their candidate for president and equal in number to that State's electoral vote. The voters of each State would then vote for each individual listed in the slate of whichever party's candidate they preferred. Yet the business of presenting separate party slates of individuals occasionally led to confusion. Some voters divided their votes between party lists because of personal loyalties to the individuals involved rather than according to their choice for president. Other voters, either out of fatigue or confusion, voted for fewer than the entire party list. The result, especially in close elections, was the occasional splitting of a State's electoral vote. This happened as late as 1916 in West Virginia when seven Republican Electors and one Democrat Elector won.

Today, the individual party candidates for Elector are seldom listed on the ballot. Instead, the expression "Electors for" usually appears in fine print on the ballot in front of each set of candidates for president and vice president (or else the State law specifies that votes cast for the candidates are to be counted as being for the slate of delegates pledged to those candidates). It is still true, however, that voters are actually casting their votes for the Electors for the presidential and vice presidential candidates of their choice rather than for the candidates themselves.

## The Time of Choosing Electors

The time for choosing Electors has undergone a similar evolution. For while the Constitution specifically gives to the Congress the power to "determine the Time of chusing the Electors", the Congress at first gave some latitude to the States.

For the first fifty years of the Federation, Congress permitted the States to conduct their presidential elections (or otherwise to choose their

Electors) anytime in a 34 day period before the first Wednesday of December which was the day set for the meeting of the Electors in their respective States. The problems born of such an arrangement are obvious and were intensified by improved communications. For the States which voted later could swell, diminish, or be influenced by a candidate's victories in the States which voted earlier. In close elections, the States which voted last might well determine the outcome. (And it is perhaps for this reason that South Carolina, always among the last States to choose its Electors, maintained for so long its tradition of choosing them by the State legislature. In close elections, the South Carolina State legislature might well decide the presidency!).

The Congress, in 1845, therefore adopted a uniform day on which the States were to choose their Electors. That day -- the Tuesday following the first Monday in November in years divisible by four -- continues to be the day on which all the States now conduct their presidential elections.

## Historical Curiosities

In the evolution of the Electoral College, there have been some interesting developments and remarkable outcomes. Critics often try to use these as examples of what can go wrong. Yet most of these historical curiosities were the result of profound political divisions within the country which the designers of the Electoral College system seem to have anticipated as needing resolution at a higher level.

■ **In 1800**, as previously noted, the Democratic-Republican Electors gave both Thomas Jefferson and Aaron Burr an equal number of electoral votes. The tie, settled in Jefferson's favor by the House of Representatives in accordance with the original design of the Electoral College system, prompted the 12th Amendment which effectively prevented this sort of thing from ever happening again.

■ **In 1824**, there were four fairly strong contenders in the presidential contest (Andrew Jackson, John Quincy Adams, William Crawford, and Henry Clay) each of whom represented an important faction within the now vastly dominant Democratic-Republican Party. The electoral votes were so divided amongst them that no one received the necessary majority to become president (although the popular John C. Calhoun did receive enough electoral votes to become vice president). In accordance with the provisions of the 12th Amendment, the choice of president devolved upon the House of Representatives who narrowly selected John Quincy Adams despite the fact that Andrew Jackson had obtained the greater number of electoral votes. This election is often cited as the first one in which the candidate who obtained the greatest popular vote (Jackson) failed to be elected president. The claim is a weak one, though, since six of the twenty four States at the time still chose their Electors in the State legislature. Some of these (such as sizable New York) would likely have returned large majorities for Adams had they conducted a popular election.

■ **The 1836** presidential election was a truly strange event. The developing Whig Party, for example, decided to run three different presidential candidates (William Henry Harrison, Daniel Webster, and Hugh White) in separate parts of the country. The idea was that their respective regional popularities would ensure a Whig majority in the Electoral College which would then decide on a single Whig presidential ticket. This fairly inspired scheme failed, though, when Democratic-Republican candidate Martin Van Buren won an absolute majority of Electors. Nor has such a strategy ever again been seriously attempted. Yet Van Buren himself did not escape the event entirely unscathed. For while he obtained an electoral majority, his vice presidential running mate (one Richard Johnson) was considered so objectionable by some of the Democratic-Republican Electors that he failed to obtain the necessary majority of electoral votes to become vice president. In accordance with the 12th Amendment, the decision devolved upon the Senate which chose Johnson as vice president anyway. A really bizarre election, that one.

■ **In the 1872** election, Democratic candidate Horace Greeley (he of earlier "Go West, young man, go West" journalistic fame whose nomination makes a good story in itself) thoughtlessly died during that period between the popular vote for Electors and the meeting of the Electoral College. The Electors who were pledged to him, clearly unprepared for such an eventuality, split their electoral votes amongst several other Democratic candidates (including three votes for Greeley himself as a possible comment on the incumbent Ulysses S. Grant). That hardly mattered, though, since the Republican Grant had readily won an absolute majority of Electors. Still, it was an interesting event for which the political parties are now prepared.

■ **In 1876,** the country once again found itself in serious political turmoil echoing, in some respects, both the economic divisions of 1824 and the impending political party realignments of 1836, but with the added bitterness of Reconstruction. A number of deep cross currents were in play. After a vast economic expansion, the country had fallen into a deep depression. Monetary and tariff issues were eroding the Union Republican coalition of East and West while a solid Republican black vote eroded the traditional Democratic hold on the South. The incumbent Republican administration of Grant had suffered a seemingly endless series of scandals involving graft and corruption on a scale hitherto unknown. And the South was eager to put an end to Radical Reconstruction which was, after all, a kind of vast political mugging. Against this backdrop, the resurging Democratic Party easily nominated Samuel J. Tilden, the popular Governor of New York, and Thomas A. Hendricks of Indiana (shrewd geographic choices under the circumstances). The Republicans, in a more turbulent convention, selected Ohio Governor Rutherford B. Hayes and William A. Wheeler of New York. A variety of fairly significant third parties also cropped up, further shattering the country's political cohesion.

This is about as good a prescription for electoral chaos as anyone might hope for. Indeed, it is almost surprising that things did not turn out worse than they did. For on election night, it looked as though Tilden had pulled off the first Democratic presidential victory since the Civil War -- although the decisive electoral votes of South Carolina, Florida, and Louisiana remained in balance. Yet these States were as divided internally as was the nation at large. Without detailing the machinations of the vote count, suffice it to say that each State finally delivered to the Congress two sets of electoral votes --one set for Tilden and one set for Hayes. Because the Congressional procedures for resolving disputed sets of Electors had expired, the Congress established a special 15-member commission to decide the issue in each of the three States. After much partisan intrigue, the special commission decided (by one vote in each case) on Hayes' Electors from all three States. Thus, Hayes was elected president despite the fact that Tilden, by everyone's count, had obtained a slight majority of popular votes (although the difference was a mere 3% of the total vote cast). As a final note, the Congress enacted in 1887 legislation that delegated to each State the final authority to determine the legality of its choice of Electors and required a concurrent majority of both houses of Congress to reject any electoral vote. That legislation remains in effect to this day so that the events of 1876 will not repeat themselves.

■ Benjamin Harrison's election in **1888** is really the only clearcut instance in which the Electoral College vote went contrary to the popular vote. This happened because the incumbent, Democrat Grover Cleveland, ran up huge popular majorities in several of the 18 States which supported him while the Republican challenger, Benjamin Harrison, won only slender majorities in some of the larger of the 20 States which supported him (most notably in Cleveland's home State of New York). Even so, the difference between them was only 110,476 votes out of 11,381,032 cast -- less than 1% of the total. Interestingly, in this case, there were few critical issues (other than tariffs) separating the candidates so that the election seems to have been fought -- and won -- more on the basis of superior party organization in getting out the vote than on the issues of the day.

These, then, are the major historical curiosities of the Electoral College system. And because they are so frequently cited as flaws in the system, a few observations on them seem in order.

First, all of these events occurred over a century ago. For the past hundred years, the Electoral College has functioned without incident in every presidential election through two world wars, a major economic depression, and several periods of acute civil unrest. Only twice in this century (the States' Rights Democrats in 1948 and George Wallace's American Independents in 1968) have there been attempts to block an Electoral College victory and thus either force a negotiation for the presidency or else force the decision into the Congress. Neither attempt came close to succeeding. Such stability, rare in human history, should not be lightly dismissed.

Second, each of these events (except 1888) resulted either from political inexperience (as in 1800, 1836, and 1872) or from profound political divisions within the country (as in 1824, 1876, and even 1948 and 1968) which required some sort of higher order political resolution. And all of them were resolved in a peaceable and orderly fashion without any public uprising and without endangering the legitimacy of the sitting president. Indeed, it is hard to imagine how a direct election of the president could have resolved events as agreeably.

Finally, as the election of 1888 demonstrates, the Electoral College system imposes two requirements on candidates for the presidency:

that the victor obtain a *sufficient* popular vote to enable him to govern (although this may not be the absolute majority), and

that such a popular vote be sufficiently *distributed* across the country to enable him to govern.

Such an arrangement ensures a regional balance of support which is a vital consideration in governing a large and diverse nation (even though in close elections, as in 1888, distribution of support may take precedence over majority of support).

Far from being flaws, then, the historical oddities described above demonstrate the strength and resilience of the Electoral College system in being able to select a president in even the most troubled of times.

## Current Workings of the Electoral College

The current workings of the Electoral College are the result of both design and experience. As it now operates:

Each State is allocated a number of Electors equal to the number of its U.S. Senators (always 2) plus the number of its U.S. Representatives (which may change each decade according to the size of each State's population as determined in the Census).

- The political parties (or independent candidates) in each State submit to the State's chief election official a list of individuals pledged to their candidate for president and equal in number to the State's electoral vote. Usually, the major political parties select these individuals either in their State party conventions or through appointment by their State party leaders while third parties and independent candidates merely designate theirs.

- Members of Congress and employees of the federal government are prohibited from serving as an Elector in order to maintain the balance between the legislative and executive branches of the federal government.

- After their caucuses and primaries, the major parties nominate their candidates for president and vice president in their national conventions -- traditionally held in the summer preceding the election. (Third parties and independent candidates follow different procedures according to the individual State laws). The names of the duly nominated candidates are then officially submitted to each State's chief election official so that they might appear on the general election ballot.

- On the Tuesday following the first Monday of November in years divisible by four, the people in each State cast their ballots for the party slate of Electors representing their choice for president and vice president (although as a matter of practice, general election ballots normally say "Electors for" each set of candidates rather than list the individual Electors on each slate).

- Whichever party slate wins the most popular votes in the State becomes that State's Electors -- so that, in effect, whichever presidential ticket gets the most popular votes in a State wins all the Electors of that State. [The two exceptions to this are Maine and Nebraska where two Electors are chosen by statewide popular vote and the remainder by the popular vote within each Congressional district].

- On the Monday following the second Wednesday of December (as established in federal law) each State's Electors meet in their respective State capitals and cast their electoral votes -- one for president and one for vice president.

- In order to prevent Electors from voting only for "favorite sons" of their home State, at least one of their votes must be for a person from outside their State (though this is seldom a problem since the parties have consistently nominated presidential and vice presidential candidates from different States).

- The electoral votes are then sealed and transmitted from each State to the President of the Senate who, on the following January 6, opens and reads them before both houses of the Congress.

- The candidate for president with the most electoral votes, provided that it is an absolute majority (one over half of the total), is declared president. Similarly, the vice presidential candidate with the absolute majority of electoral votes is declared vice president.

- In the event no one obtains an absolute majority of electoral votes for president, the U.S. House of Representatives (as the chamber closest to the people) selects the president from among the top three contenders with each State casting only one vote and an absolute majority of the States being required to elect. Similarly, if no one obtains an absolute majority for vice president, then the U.S. Senate makes the selection from among the top two contenders for that office.

- At noon on January 20, the duly elected president and vice president are sworn into office.

Occasionally questions arise about what would happen if the presidential or vice presidential candidate died at some point in this process. For answers to these, as well as to a number of other "what if" questions, readers are advised to consult a small volume entitled *After the People Vote: Steps in Choosing the President* edited by Walter Berns and published in 1983 by the American Enterprise Institute. Similarly, further details on the history and current functioning of the Electoral College are available in the second edition of Congressional Quarterly's *Guide to U.S. Elections*, a real goldmine of information, maps, and statistics.

# The Pro's and Con's of the Electoral College System

There have, in its 200-year history, been a number of critics and proposed reforms to the Electoral College system -- most of them trying to eliminate it. But there are also staunch defenders of the Electoral College who, though perhaps less vocal than its critics, offer very powerful arguments in its favor.

### Arguments Against the Electoral College

Those who object to the Electoral College system and favor a direct popular election of the president generally do so on four grounds:

- the possibility of electing a minority president

- the risk of so-called "faithless" Electors,

■ the possible role of the Electoral College in depressing voter turnout, and

■ its failure to accurately reflect the national popular will.

Opponents of the Electoral College are disturbed by ***the possibility of electing a minority president*** (one without the absolute majority of popular votes). Nor is this concern entirely unfounded since there are three ways in which that could happen.

One way in which a minority president could be elected is if the country were so deeply divided politically that three or more presidential candidates split the electoral votes among them such that no one obtained the necessary majority. This occurred, as noted above, in 1824 and was unsuccessfully attempted in 1948 and again in 1968. Should that happen today, there are two possible resolutions: either one candidate could throw his electoral votes to the support of another (before the meeting of the Electors) or else, absent an absolute majority in the Electoral College, the U.S. House of Representatives would select the president in accordance with the 12th Amendment. Either way, though, the person taking office would not have obtained the absolute majority of the popular vote. Yet it is unclear how a direct election of the president could resolve such a deep national conflict without introducing a presidential run-off election -- a procedure which would add substantially to the time, cost, and effort already devoted to selecting a president and which might well deepen the political divisions while trying to resolve them.

A second way in which a minority president could take office is if, as in 1888, one candidate's popular support were heavily concentrated in a few States while the other candidate maintained a slim popular lead in enough States to win the needed majority of the Electoral College. While the country has occasionally come close to this sort of outcome, the question here is whether the **distribution** of a candidate's popular support should be taken into account alongside the relative size of it. This issue was mentioned above and is discussed at greater length below.

A third way of electing a minority president is if a third party or candidate, however small, drew enough votes from the top two that no one received over 50% of the national popular total. Far from being unusual, this sort of thing has, in fact, happened 15 times including (in this century) Wilson in both 1912 and 1916, Truman in 1948, Kennedy in 1960, Nixon in 1968, and Clinton in both 1992 1nd 1996. The only remarkable thing about those outcomes is that few people noticed and even fewer cared. Nor would a direct election have changed those outcomes without a run-off requiring over 50% of the popular vote (an idea which not even proponents of a direct election seem to advocate).

Opponents of the Electoral College system also point to ***the risk of so-called "faithless" Electors***. A "faithless Elector" is one who is pledged to vote for his party's candidate for president but nevertheless votes for another candidate. There have been 7 such Electors in this century and as recently as 1988 when a Democrat Elector in the State of West Virginia cast his votes for Lloyd Bensen for president and Michael Dukakis for vice president instead of the other way around. Faithless Electors have never changed the outcome of an election, though, simply because most often their purpose is to make a statement rather than make a difference. That is to say, when the electoral vote outcome is so obviously going to be for one candidate or the other, an occasional Elector casts a vote for some personal favorite knowing full well that it will not make a difference in the result. Still, if the prospect of a faithless Elector is so fearsome as to warrant a Constitutional amendment, then it is possible to solve the problem without abolishing the Electoral College merely by eliminating the individual Electors in favor of a purely mathematical process (since the individual Electors are no longer essential to its operation).

Opponents of the Electoral College are further concerned about *its possible role in depressing voter turnout*. Their argument is that, since each State is entitled to the same number of electoral votes regardless of its voter turnout, there is no incentive in the States to encourage voter participation. Indeed, there may even be an incentive to discourage participation (and they often cite the South here) so as to enable a minority of citizens to decide the electoral vote for the whole State. While this argument has a certain surface plausibility, it fails to account for the fact that presidential elections do not occur in a vacuum. States also conduct other elections (for U.S. Senators, U.S. Representatives, State Governors, State legislators, and a host of local officials) in which these same incentives and disincentives are likely to operate, if at all, with an even greater force. It is hard to imagine what counter-incentive would be created by eliminating the Electoral College.

Finally, some opponents of the Electoral College point out, quite correctly, *its failure to accurately reflect the national popular will* in at least two respects.

First, the distribution of Electoral votes in the College tends to over-represent people in rural States. This is because the number of Electors for each State is determined by the number of members it has in the House (which more or less reflects the State's population size) **plus** the number of members it has in the Senate (which is always two regardless of the State's population). The result is that in 1988, for example, the combined voting age population (3,119,000) of the seven least populous jurisdictions of Alaska, Delaware, the District of Columbia, North Dakota, South Dakota, Vermont, and Wyoming carried the same voting strength in the Electoral College (21 Electoral votes) as the 9,614,000 persons of voting age in the State of Florida. Each Floridian's potential vote, then, carried about one third the weight of a potential vote in the other States listed.

A second way in which the Electoral College fails to accurately reflect the national popular will stems primarily from the winner-take-all mechanism whereby the presidential candidate who wins the most popular votes in the State wins all the Electoral votes of that State. One effect of this mechanism is to make it extremely difficult for third-party or independent candidates ever to make much of a showing in the Electoral College. If, for example, a third-party or independent candidate were to win the support of even as many as 25% of the voters nationwide, he might still end up with no Electoral College votes at all unless he won a plurality of votes in at least one State. And even if he managed to win a few States, his support elsewhere would not be reflected. By thus failing to accurately reflect the national popular will, the argument goes, the Electoral College reinforces a two-party system, discourages third-party or independent candidates, and thereby tends to restrict choices available to the electorate.

In response to these arguments, proponents of the Electoral College point out that it was never intended to reflect the national popular will. As for the first issue, that the Electoral College over-represents rural populations, proponents respond that the United States Senate -- with two seats per State regardless of its population -- over-represents rural populations far more dramatically. But since there have been no serious proposals to abolish the United States Senate on these grounds, why should such an argument be used to abolish the lesser case of the Electoral College? Because the presidency represents the whole country? But so, as an institution, does the United States Senate.

As for the second issue of the Electoral College's role in reinforcing a two-party system, proponents, as we shall see, find this to be a positive virtue.

## Arguments for the Electoral College

Proponents of the Electoral College system normally defend it on the philosophical grounds that it:

- contributes to the cohesiveness of the country by requiring a distribution of popular support to be elected president

- enhances the status of minority interests,

- contributes to the political stability of the nation by encouraging a two-party system, and

- maintains a federal system of government and representation.

Recognizing the strong regional interests and loyalties which have played so great a role in American history, proponents argue that the Electoral College system *contributes to the cohesiveness of the country*

***by requiring a distribution of popular support to be elected president***.
Without such a mechanism, they point out, presidents would be selected
either through the domination of one populous region over the others or
through the domination of large metropolitan areas over the rural ones.
Indeed, it is principally because of the Electoral College that presidential
nominees are inclined to select vice presidential running mates from a
region other than their own. For as things stand now, no one region
contains the absolute majority (270) of electoral votes required to elect a
president. Thus, there is an incentive for presidential candidates to pull
together coalitions of States and regions rather than to exacerbate regional
differences. Such a unifying mechanism seems especially prudent in view
of the severe regional problems that have typically plagued geographically
large nations such as China, India, the Soviet Union, and even, in its time,
the Roman Empire.

This unifying mechanism does not, however, come without a small
price. And the price is that in very close popular elections, it is possible that
the candidate who wins a slight majority of popular votes may not be the
one elected president -- depending (as in 1888) on whether his popularity is
concentrated in a few States or whether it is more evenly distributed across
the States. Yet this is less of a problem than it seems since, as a practical
matter, the popular difference between the two candidates would likely be so
small that either candidate could govern effectively.

Proponents thus believe that the practical value of requiring a
distribution of popular support outweighs whatever sentimental value may
attach to obtaining a bare majority of the popular support. Indeed, they
point out that the Electoral College system is designed to work in a rational
series of defaults: if, in the first instance, a candidate receives a substantial
majority of the popular vote, then that candidate is virtually certain to win
enough electoral votes to be elected president; in the event that the popular
vote is extremely close, then the election defaults to that candidate with the
best distribution of popular votes (as evidenced by obtaining the absolute
majority of electoral votes); in the event the country is so divided that no one
obtains an absolute majority of electoral votes, then the choice of president
defaults to the States in the U.S. House of Representatives. One way or
another, then, the winning candidate must demonstrate both a **sufficient**
popular support to govern as well as a sufficient **distribution** of that
support to govern.

Proponents also point out that, far from diminishing minority
interests by depressing voter participation, the Electoral College actually
***enhances the status of minority groups***. This is so because the votes of
even small minorities in a State may make the difference between winning
**all** of that State's electoral votes or **none** of that State's electoral votes. And
since ethnic minority groups in the United States happen to concentrate in
those States with the most electoral votes, they assume an importance to
presidential candidates well out of proportion to their number. The same

principle applies to other special interest groups such as labor unions, farmers, environmentalists, and so forth.

It is because of this "leverage effect" that the presidency, as an institution, tends to be more sensitive to ethnic minority and other special interest groups than does the Congress as an institution. Changing to a direct election of the president would therefore actually damage minority interests since their votes would be overwhelmed by a national popular majority.

Proponents further argue that the Electoral College **contributes to the political stability of the nation** by encouraging a two-party system. There can be no doubt that the Electoral College has encouraged and helps to maintain a two- party system in the United States. This is true simply because it is extremely difficult for a new or minor party to win enough popular votes in enough States to have a chance of winning the presidency. Even if they won enough electoral votes to force the decision into the U.S. House of Representatives, they would still have to have a majority of over half the State delegations in order to elect their candidate -- and in that case, they would hardly be considered a minor party.

In addition to protecting the presidency from impassioned but transitory third party movements, the practical effect of the Electoral College (along with the single-member district system of representation in the Congress) is to virtually force third party movements into one of the two major political parties. Conversely, the major parties have every incentive to absorb minor party movements in their continual attempt to win popular majorities in the States. In this process of assimilation, third party movements are obliged to compromise their more radical views if they hope to attain any of their more generally acceptable objectives. Thus we end up with two large, pragmatic political parties which tend to the center of public opinion rather than dozens of smaller political parties catering to divergent and sometimes extremist views. In other words, such a system forces political coalitions to occur within the political parties rather than within the government.

A direct popular election of the president would likely have the opposite effect. For in a direct popular election, there would be every incentive for a multitude of minor parties to form in an attempt to prevent whatever popular majority might be necessary to elect a president. The surviving candidates would thus be drawn to the regionalist or extremist views represented by these parties in hopes of winning the run-off election.

The result of a direct popular election for president, then, would likely be a frayed and unstable political system characterized by a multitude of political parties and by more radical changes in policies from one administration to the next. The Electoral College system, in contrast, encourages political parties to coalesce divergent interests into two sets of coherent alternatives. Such an organization of social conflict and political debate contributes to the political stability of the nation.

Finally, its proponents argue quite correctly that the Electoral College *maintains a federal system of government and representation*. Their reasoning is that in a formal federal structure, important political powers are reserved to the component States. In the United States, for example, the House of Representatives was designed to represent the States according to the size of their population. The States are even responsible for drawing the district lines for their House seats. The Senate was designed to represent each State equally regardless of its population. And the Electoral College was designed to represent each State's choice for the presidency (with the number of each State's electoral votes being the number of its Senators plus the number of its Representatives). To abolish the Electoral College in favor of a nationwide popular election for president would strike at the very heart of the federal structure laid out in our Constitution and would lead to the nationalization of our central government -- to the detriment of the States.

Indeed, if we become obsessed with government by popular majority as the only consideration, should we not then abolish the Senate which represents States regardless of population? Should we not correct the minor distortions in the House (caused by districting and by guaranteeing each State at least one Representative) by changing it to a system of proportional representation? This would accomplish "government by popular majority" and guarantee the representation of minority parties, but it would also demolish our federal system of government. If there are reasons to maintain State representation in the Senate and House as they exist today, then surely these same reasons apply to the choice of president. Why, then, apply a sentimental attachment to popular majorities only to the Electoral College?

The fact is, they argue, that the original design of our federal system of government was thoroughly and wisely debated by the Founding Fathers. State viewpoints, they decided, are more important than political minority viewpoints. And the collective opinion of the individual State populations is more important than the opinion of the national population taken as a whole. Nor should we tamper with the careful balance of power between the national and State governments which the Founding Fathers intended and which is reflected in the Electoral College. To do so would fundamentally alter the nature of our government and might well bring about consequences that even the reformers would come to regret.

## Conclusion

The Electoral College has performed its function for over 200 years (and in over 50 presidential elections) by ensuring that the President of the United States has both sufficient popular support to govern and that his popular support is sufficiently distributed throughout the country to enable him to govern effectively.

Although there were a few anomalies in its early history, none have occurred in the past century.  Proposals to abolish the Electoral College, though frequently put forward, have failed  largely because the alternatives to it appear more problematic than is the College itself.

The fact that the Electoral College was originally designed to solve one set of problems but today serves to solve an  entirely different set of problems is a tribute to the genius of  the Founding Fathers and to the durability of the American federal system.

# A Selected Bibliography on the Electoral College

## Highly Recommended

Berns, Walter (ed.). *After the People Vote: Steps in Choosing the President.* Washington: American Enterprise Institute for Public Policy Research, 1983.

Bickel, Alexander M. *Reform and Continuity.* New York: Harper & Row, 1971.

Glennon, Michael J. *When No Majority Rules: The Electoral College and Presidential Succession.* Washington D.C.: Congressional Quarterly, 1992.

*Congressional Quarterly's Guide to U.S. Elections* (2nd ed.). Washington, D.C.: Congressional Quarterly, 1985.

Schlesinger, Arthur M. Jr.(ed.). *History of Presidential Elections 1789-1968.* New York: Chelsea House Publishers, 1971.

## Other Sources

American Enterprise Institute for Public Policy Research. *Proposals for Revision of the Electoral College System.* Washington: 1969.

Best, Judith. *The Case Against the Direct Election of the President.* Ithica: Cornell University Press, 1975.

Longley, Lawrence D. *The Politics of Electoral College Reform.* New Haven: Yale University Press, 1972.

Pierce, Neal R. and Longley, Lawrence D. *The People's President: The Electoral College in American History and the Direct-Vote Alternative.* New Haven: Yale University Press, 1981.

Sayre, Wallace Stanley. *Voting for President.* Washington: Brookings Institution, c1970.

Zeidenstein, Harvey G. *Direct Election of the President.* Lexington, Mass: Lexington Books, 1973.